Fact Finders®

FULL STEAM FOOTBALL

Science, Technology, Engineering, Arts, and Mathematics of the Game

by Sean McCollum

CAPSTONE PRESS
a capstone imprint

Fact Finders Books are published by Capstone Press
1710 Roe Crest Drive, North Mankato, Minnesota 56003

www.mycapstone.com

Library of Congress Cataloging-in-Publication Data
Names: McCollum, Sean, author.
Title: Full STEAM football : science, technology, engineering, arts, and mathematics
of the game / by Sean McCollum.
Description: North Mankato, Minnesota : Capstone Press, 2019. | Series: Fact finders.
Full STEAM sports | Audience: Age 8–14.
Identifiers: LCCN 2018016134 (print) | LCCN 2018019631 (ebook) | ISBN 9781543530476
(eBook PDF) | ISBN 9781543530391 (hardcover) | ISBN 9781543530438 (pbk.)
Subjects: LCSH: Football—Juvenile literature. | Sports sciences—Juvenile literature. |
Sports—Technological innovations—Juvenile literature. Classification: LCC GV950.7
(ebook) | LCC GV950.7 .M335 2019 (print) | DDC 796.332—dc23
LC record available at https://lccn.loc.gov/2018016134

Editorial Credits
Editor: Nate LeBoutillier
Designer: Terri Poburka
Media Researcher: Eric Gohl
Production Specialist: Kris Wilfahrt

Photo Credits
AP Photo: John Froschauer, 14, Paul Sancya, 10; Dreamstime: Jerry Coli, 19 (top right);
Getty Images: Boston Globe, 13, Carlos M. Saavedra, 17, Thearon W. Henderson, 20;
Library of Congress: 18 (right); Newscom: Cal Sport Media/Chris Szagola, 19 (middle
right), Cal Sport Media/Duncan Williams, 8, Cal Sport Media/Jevone Moore, cover, Cal
Sport Media/John Mersits, 9, Cal Sport Media/Tim Warner, 15, Icon Sportswire/Daniel
Gluskoter, 22, Icon Sportswire/Jeffrey Brown, 23 (bottom), Icon Sportswire/Nick
Wosika, 27, Icon Sportswire/Shelley Lipton, 28, KRT/Hulteng, 18 (helmets), 19 (top five
helmets), MCT/Jeff Siner, 24, TNS/Al Diaz, 11, TNS/LiPo Ching, 12, TNS/Paul Moseley,
7, UPI/Matthew Healey, 4, USA Today Sports/Joe Nicholson, 19 (bottom right), USA
Today Sports/Reuters, 21, ZUMA Press/The Washington Times, 25; Shutterstock: Todd
Taulman Photography, 19 (bottom helmet); Wikimedia: Public Domain, 23 (top)

Design Elements
Shutterstock

Printed and bound in the USA.
PA017

CONTENTS

STEAM ON THE GRIDIRON

Football players strap on helmets, line up, and wait for the kicker to blast the ball. Then two teams race at each other like charging bulls. The sport of football features speed and force. Football players and coaches use the latest gear, equipment, and training systems. They work to be the best. With the help of science, technology, engineering, the arts, and mathematics (STEAM), players and teams set records and have winning seasons.

CHAPTER ONE

SCIENCE

PHYSICS: Throwing a Spiral Pass

A quarterback cocks his arm and sends the football into the air. The ball spirals and spins toward its target. Why is the spiral throw the best way to throw a football? The science of physics explains it.

In most sports, balls are round spheres. But a football is not. Spinning the egg-shaped ball on its long **axis** does two things as the football flies. First, spin decreases air resistance, or **drag**. The football cuts through the air better.

axis—a real or imaginary line through the center of an object, around which the object turns

drag—the force created when air strikes and slows a moving object

Quarterbacks throw spiral passes.

Second, a spiral has **angular momentum**. A spinning top is a good example of this force. The faster a top spins the more stable it is. As it slows down, it starts to wobble. The same is true for a spiraling football. The faster it spins, the more likely it is to head straight to its target.

angular momentum—the amount of force in an object moving at an angle determined by the object's mass and speed

D efensive players use a force called **torque**. In physics, torque is energy used to make something rotate or spin. A player uses torque when he makes a tackle.

Crouching down allows a player to tackle another player below his center of mass.

Tackling at the center of mass makes it harder to knock a player off his feet.

A player has a **center of mass**. It is the point in a body at which most of the weight is concentrated. If a player is tackled at his center of mass, it is hard to knock him down. But if a defensive player tackles below the center of mass, it causes a rotational force. The other player's feet rotate or turn into the air. The rotation is caused by torque. The player loses his balance and falls to the ground.

torque—the force that causes rotation around an axis

center of mass—the point in a body at which most of the weight is located; below that point, a body is easier to topple

A wide receiver hits the field headfirst after diving for a pass. He may have suffered a **concussion**. A concussion is a brain injury. It can cause headaches and **memory** loss.

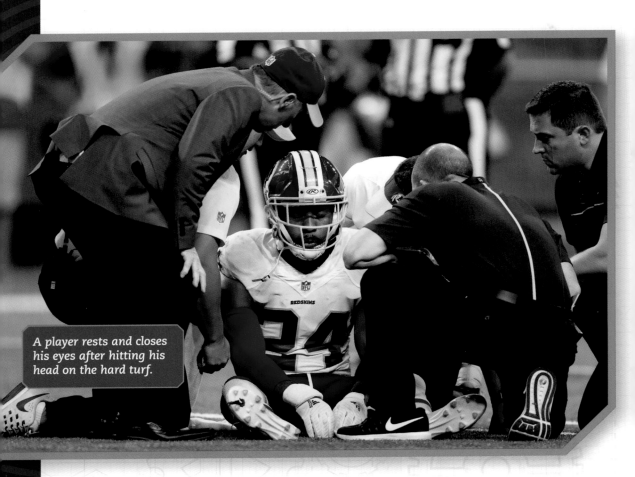

A player rests and closes his eyes after hitting his head on the hard turf.

Scientists study how concussions affect players, even long after they have quit football. Brain studies of former players show many had a brain disease. It is called chronic traumatic encephalopathy (CTE). CTE can cause problems with memory, mood, speech, and eyesight. Experts think repeated hits to a person's head causes CTE.

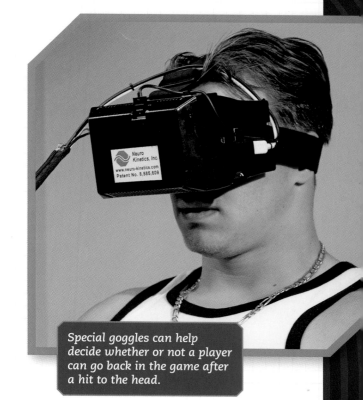

Special goggles can help decide whether or not a player can go back in the game after a hit to the head.

The studies make football teams take concussions more seriously. Coaches, trainers, and doctors use better tests to check for concussions. If a player gets one, total rest is the only treatment. Science is helping make the game safer for players.

concussion—an injury to the brain caused by a hard blow to the head
memory—the power to remember things

CHAPTER TWO

TECHNOLOGY

COMPUTER TECHNOLOGY: Virtual Practice

I n 2017 the University of Alabama Crimson Tide led the Clemson University Tigers, 24-14. To protect their lead, the Crimson Tide rushed at Tigers quarterback Deshaun Watson again and again.

The STRIVR virtual reality training system gives players the feeling they are in a real game.

A player uses a virtual reality headset during a training camp in 2016.

Watson, though, had practiced against Alabama many times. He had used virtual reality. Virtual reality (VR) is a computer technology. He wore a headset with goggles to practice against a video version of the Tide. VR is somewhat like a video game. For Watson, the VR experience was lifelike. In the real game, he played like he had seen it all before.

Many football teams use virtual reality in their training. It lets players practice without getting hurt.

Coaches on the sidelines or in press boxes high above the field call plays for quarterbacks to run. These coaches call in plays using helmet radios.

In the 1950s, head coach Paul Brown experimented with a radio helmet. But his quarterback complained he was hearing radio calls from taxi drivers near the stadium. Thankfully technology improved.

In 1994 the NFL allowed teams to put radio receivers inside quarterback helmets. Beginning in 2008, one player on defense was also allowed to receive play calls from the bench.

A quarterback uses a tablet to review plays.

The radio system is tested before each game. Officials make sure each team has a secure **radio frequency**. Otherwise the other team might steal the signals. During the game, coaches call plays. Signal-callers then relay the plays to their teammates before the ball is snapped.

A quarterback listens to a play call inside his helmet during a game.

radio frequency—the waves used in radio communication

Technology worn by players helps test their biomechanics. Biomechanics is the study of how players move. For example, the motusQB company made a high-tech arm sleeve. It measures the movements of a quarterback's throw. Coaches and players can use the data to improve play.

Athletic trainers use biometric **monitors** to track player conditioning. Players can wear devices on their wrists to measure their heart rate. Some teams have players swallow "radio pills." These devices keep track of body heat during hot practices. It helps keep players from overheating and getting sick.

monitor—a device that shows information

Zebra Technologies employees watch computer screens to track players.

Teamwork gets a boost from Zebra Technologies. This company puts a small radio frequency identification (RFID) tag in each shoulder pad. Sensors map where players are on the field during every second of play. Coaches use the information to study if players are moving to the right place at the right time.

CHAPTER THREE

ENGINEERING

SAFETY ENGINEERING:
The Football Helmet

E ngineering is the use of science, technology, mathematics, and other knowledge to fix problems. With football helmets, engineering has focused on keeping the head safer.

1937

Early 1900s
Some college players start wearing soft leather skull caps.

1920s-1930s
The National Football League starts in 1920. More players start using hard leather helmets. Players are nicknamed "leatherheads."

1939
John T. Riddell company introduces the plastic helmet. Some players add cotton padding to the inside.

1940
The chin strap is introduced.

1943
All NFL players must wear helmets.

1948
Fred Gehrke of the Los Angeles Rams paints horns on his helmet. It's the first helmet emblem.

1955
The single-bar facemask is first used.

1960s
Thick foam padding is added to helmets. Players start wearing double-bar face masks.

1970s
The full face mask becomes standard equipment.

1986
Stronger polycarbonate shells replace plastic.

1994
Helmet radios are introduced for quarterbacks.

1998
Clear eye visors are permitted for the first time.

2017
The Zero1 helmet is worn in games by QB Russell Wilson and other NFL players for the first time. The four-layer helmet is made to better protect heads.

1970s

2012

2017

In a 2014 game, Odell Beckham Jr. of the New York Giants made a great catch. Twisting as he dove backward, the receiver extended one hand. The ball stuck to his fingers like steel to a magnet.

Beckham Jr.'s big hands are one secret weapon. His gloves are another. The secret to the gloves lies in materials engineering. This field of engineering creates new materials for every purpose.

How do football gloves work? Most gloves are made from thin leather and artificial fabrics. The palms and fingers are then treated with a material called silicone. Compared to bare hands, these gloves can triple the friction with a football.

Gloves grip the ball.

Odell Beckham Jr. made an amazing catch thanks in part to his gloves.

Friction is a force created when two objects rub against each other. Friction slows objects down. Push a sneaker across a table. Now try a dress shoe. Whichever slides easier has less friction. When it comes to gloves, more friction means better grip.

CHAPTER FOUR

ARTS

FASHION DESIGN:
Football Flair

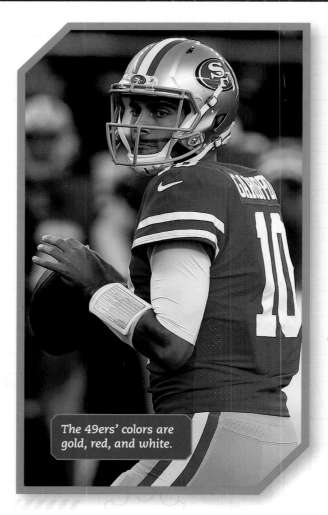

The 49ers' colors are gold, red, and white.

P layers and fans wear their team's colors and **logos** with pride. Behind many team colors, mascots, and uniforms is a story. Often history combines with art in sports fashion. For example, the San Francisco 49ers name and golden helmets represent the city's history. Thousands of people came to San Francisco in search of gold in 1849. Those people were called 49ers.

logo—a visual symbol of a company

The Baltimore Ravens mascot comes from literature. It honors author Edgar Allan Poe and his famous poem "The Raven." The team's purple-and-black colors reflect that bird's feathers. Poe died and is buried in Baltimore.

Edgar Allan Poe

A raven is on Baltimore's helmet.

In the early 1960s, filmmaker Ed Sabol and his son Steve used the arts to explain football to new fans. Their football films turned games into stories. They put microphones on coaches.

Cameras capture moments of the game.

Steve Sabol standing next to millions of feet of NFL film in 2002.

They used cameras to zoom in for close-ups of players' faces. **Slow-motion** shots captured long bombs spiraling through the air. The Sabols added music and a narrator to explain the action.

The Sabols' company, NFL Films, showed the beauty and toughness of the game. The films turned football stars into heroes. The Sabols also produced "**blooper** reels" that showed football's funny side. The Sabols' work helped turn the NFL into the popular sport it is today.

slow-motion—the action of showing film or playing back video more slowly than it was recorded, so that the action appears slower than in real life

blooper—a funny mistake caught on film

CHAPTER FIVE

MATHEMATICS

PROBABILITY: Go For It!

Imagine you're the head coach of the Green Bay Packers. Your team is down by two points with 1:23 left in the game. Your offense faces a fourth down and one yard to go at the Minnesota Vikings 41-yard line. You have no timeouts left. Do you try for a first down? Punt and try to pin the Vikings near the goal line? Or do you attempt a field goal kick? **Statistics** and **probability** can help you make the decision.

Statistics and probability are parts of mathematics. In sports, statistics measure performance, like the number of field goals a kicker has made. Probability measures the chances something will happen. Flip a coin. The chances it will come up heads is 50 percent. Tails is also 50 percent.

---

statistic—a fact shown as a number or percentage
probability—how likely or unlikely it is for something to happen

A head coach thinks of the probabilities. If you punt, there's a chance the Vikings will run out the clock and win. A field goal could win the game. But there's a chance the kicker will miss the long field goal. Should you go for the first down? Teams that went for it on 4th down in the most recent postseason had about a 60 percent success rate. What decision gives you the best probability of winning the game?

The distance from the goal is one factor in a kicker's chances of completing a field goal.

Running back Le'Veon Bell of the Pittsburgh Steelers plants his foot and turns. He dashes up the sideline. Across the field, New England Patriots cornerback Malcolm Butler turns and takes off. Now it's a race for the end zone.

Le'Veon Bell speeds toward the end zone with the football.

Butler chooses the best angle of pursuit. This angle gives him the best chance to catch Bell before he scores.

A defender chasing the ball carrier is **geometry** in action. The play uses the Pythagorean Theorem. The **theorem** relates to a right triangle. It's a triangle with one 90-degree angle.

The mathematical formula for the theorem is $a^2 + b^2 = c^2$. It allows us to figure out how far Butler has to run to knock Bell out of bounds. Let's say Bell is 40 yards from the end zone. Butler starts his chase from 30 yards away. Using the formula, we get:

$40^2 + 30^2 = c^2$

$(40 \times 40) + (30 \times 30) = c^2$

$1,600 + 900 = c^2$

$2,500 = c^2$ (or 50×50)

$50 = c$

In other words, Butler must sprint 50 yards to catch Bell before the goal line. Can he do it? Plays like these bring football fans to their feet.

geometry—a branch of mathematics that deals with lines, angles, and shapes

theorem—a statement in mathematics that can be proven to be true

GLOSSARY

angular momentum (ANG-gyu-lar moh-MEN-tuhm)—the amount of force in an object moving at an angle determined by the object's mass and speed

axis (AK-siss)—a real or imaginary line through the center of an object, around which the object turns

blooper (BLU-pur)—a funny mistake caught on film

center of mass (SEN-tur UHV MASS)—the point in a body at which most of the weight is located; below that point, a body is easier to topple

concussion (kuhn-KUH-shuhn)—an injury to the brain caused by a hard blow to the head

drag (DRAG)—force created when air strikes and slows a moving object

geometry (jee-OM-uh-tree)—a branch of mathematics that deals with lines, angles, and shapes

logo (LOH-goh)—a visual symbol of a company

memory (MEM-uh-ree)—the power to remember things

monitor (MON-uh-tur)—a device that shows information

probability (PROB-uh-bulh-uh-tee)—how likely or unlikely it is for something to happen

radio frequency (RAY-dee-oh FREE-kwuhn-see)—the waves used in radio communication

slow motion (SLO MO-shuhn)—the action of showing film or playing back video more slowly than it was recorded, so that the action appears slower than in real life

statistic (stuh-TISS-tik)—a fact shown as a number or percentage

theorem (THIHR-uhm)—a statement in mathematics that can be proven to be true

torque (TORK)—the force that causes rotation around an axis

READ MORE

Bethea, Nikole Brooks. *The Science of Football with Max Axiom, Super Scientist.* North Mankato, Minn.: Capstone Press, 2016.

Nagelhout, Ryan. *The Science of Football.* Sports Science. New York: PowerKids Press, 2016.

Nicolai, Gregory. *The Science of Football: The Top Ten Ways Science Affects the Game.* North Mankato, Minn.: Capstone Press/Sports Illustrated Kids, 2016.

INTERNET SITES

Use FactHound to find Internet sites related to this book.

Visit www.facthound.com

Just type in 9781543530391 and go.

Check out projects, games and lots more at
www.capstonekids.com

INDEX